Marquis Gets A Bicycle for Christmas

©2019 Dr. Mary J. Bryant
Kingdom Builders Publications, LLC
Illustrated by Eric Quzack
Special thanks to
Megan Bryant
for assisting in the editing process

About the Marquis Adventures

These series of books in the Marquis Adventures has been inspired by our youngest son whose name is Marquis (pronounced Mar-kiss). So, I dedicate this series to Marquis J. Bryant.

<u>Books in the Marquis Adventures Series</u>
Marquis Finds a Friend
ISBN 978-0-578-17290-3

Marquis Goes to the Circus
ISBN 978-0-692-15334-5

Marquis Gets a Bicycle for Christmas
ISBN 978-0-578-58063-0

This Book Belongs To

_____

Christmas was in two weeks and Marquis' Mother and Father were wondering what he would like for a present. They thought this would be a great time to get him his first bicycle.

Marquis' brother and sister got their first bicycle around the same age. They were so excited when they learned how to ride their bikes.

Now that Michael and Megan are older, they have bigger and faster bikes. They like riding their bikes to the park and that means Marquis gets left behind. Marquis would be so sad to see them ride off without him.

"I can't wait to see his little face when we give him his very first bicycle.", Mother said with a grin.

"Yes, said his Father, and it has to be red because that is his favorite color. I am going to have so much fun teaching him to ride it."

So, off to the store they went to find the perfect bicycle for Marquis.

After looking at a few bikes, they found the perfect one for him. It was a red freestyle bike with training wheels and a holder for a water bottle on the handlebar. His Dad found a big box that the bicycle would fit in perfectly. After wrapping the box, Marquis' Mom put a big red bow on it.

Soon it was Christmas day and Marquis woke up excited to find out what was waiting for him under the tree.

Everyone was so excited to see the expression on his face as he opened the big box with the red bow.

Marquis ripped the bow from the box. He looked inside the box and shouted, "It's a bicycle and it's red, my favorite color! Now I can ride to the park with Michael and Megan!"

Marquis couldn't wait to get dressed and go outside to start learning to ride his new bicycle. He was so excited he didn't even open his other presents.

His Dad took him outside and gave him his first lesson. Marquis had to put on his helmet, knee pads, and elbow pads. He didn't want to put them on at first, but his Dad said, "Safety first, son." So, Marquis gladly put them on.

He went up and down the sidewalk pedaling away. Though there were training wheels on the bike, he was catching on quickly.

After some time, the training wheels were ready to be removed. After falling a few times, Marquis became afraid to try again. His Mother took him in her arms and told him not to be afraid. She said, "Marquis, when you fall, you must get right back up and try again. You must not give up." Marquis believed his Mother.

He began to ride again, but this time when he fell, he got right back his bicycle. With his Father right by his side, he was finally able to keep his balance without falling.

Marquis looked at his mother and exclaimed, "Look Mom, I am riding!"

She clapped her hands and shouted, "Great job! I knew you could do it if you didn't give up!"

After a day of learning to ride his bicycle, Marquis was ready for bedtime. As his Mother and Father tucked him in bed, Marquis said proudly with a widest smile, "I fell off my bicycle, but I was brave and got back on it. Now, I get to ride my bicycle to the park with Michael and Megan."

"Yes, Dear. I am so proud of you." Mom said. She gave him a big hug and kiss. They said, "Good Night."

As soon as the lights were off, Marquis was fast asleep.

About the Author

Dr. Mary J. Bryant is an inspirational and children's author. She was inspired by her youngest son to write the first book, Marquis Finds a Friend. This series of books are called the Marquis Adventures.

Marquis Gets a Bicycle for Christmas is the third book in the series. She hopes to inspire children to enjoy reading at young age. These books also teach little life's lessons to children.

More can be learned about the author and her books at www.doveministry378.org